PRAYER

PRAYER

COMING OUT OF SPIRITUAL ISOLATION

PEG THOMPSON

 HAZELDEN®

Hazelden Educational Materials
Center City, Minnesota 55012-0176

©1994 by Peg Thompson
All rights reserved. Published 1994
From *Finding Your Own Spiritual Path: An Everyday
Guidebook* © 1994 by Peg Thompson,
published by Hazelden Foundation, October 1994.
Printed in the United States of America
No portion of this publication may be
reproduced in any manner without the
written permission of the publisher

ISBN: 1-56838-006-2

Editor's note
Hazelden Educational materials offers a variety of information on chemical dependency and related areas. Our publica-
tions do not necessarily represent Hazelden's programs, nor
do they officially speak for any Twelve Step organization.

The people in the stories that appear in this booklet are
composites of many individuals. Any resemblance to any one
person, living or dead, is strictly coincidental.

Acquisitions Editor: Judith Delaney
Manuscript Editor: Debora O'Donnell Tavolier
Cover design/Interior design: David Spohn
Copywriter: Alex Acker
Typesetter: Universal Press & Link, Minneapolis, Minnesota
Production Editor: Cynthia Madsen
Print Manager: Joan Seim
Printer: Rose Printing, Tallahassee, Florida
Managing Editor: Donald H. Freeman
The typeface used in this booklet is Adobe Garamond

To pray is to take notice of the wonder, to regain a sense of the mystery that animates all beings, the divine margin in all attainments.

—RABBI ABRAHAM JOSHUA HESCHEL,
QUEST FOR GOD

PRAYER:
COMING OUT OF SPIRITUAL ISOLATION

When I go trout fishing, I carry everything I need for the day in my multipocketed vest and fanny pack. I begin at a place where a river crosses a road and hike upstream on an angler's path, fishing as I go. Soon I am alone, with only the stream and the rest of nature as my companions. Fishing, I become one with my surroundings. I move carefully and quietly. At times, I pause to feast on wild raspberries or blueberries, enjoy the mating ritual of dragonflies, or drink in the fragrance of spruce trees and moss. Often, I just relax on a smooth rock in the sun, awash with the sights, scents, and sounds of the place. I feel in complete harmony with myself and all creation.

Occasionally, I encounter a dead end. For instance, a sheer cliff may block the trail, forcing me to cross the river in order to continue fishing. I know from experience that the fishing upstream will be better, because fewer anglers have traveled there. Often, I decide to make a crossing. I look for a place with shallower water and stable rocks. Sometimes I need a stout stick to help me assess the depth of the water and give me stability. Finally, I step into the water, picking my way from rock to rock as I cross.

For many of us, the spiritual journey resembles my fishing expeditions. We walk the path unhindered for a period of months or years. But at some point we reach an impasse: to grow in closeness to the divine, we know intuitively that we must begin to pray. Each of us comes to this crossing in our own time and in our own way, but for most of us, it is a crossing. We may have to feel our fear or anger in order to explore prayer. We may have to reevaluate outdated ideas about it. We may have to ask for help or expose our lack of experience.

Sometimes I decide not to make the crossing. If the water is too swift or too deep, or if I am tired or the hour is late, I remember the spot and return to it at another time when the currents are gentler or my energy higher. Similarly, you need not force yourself to explore prayer.

You can trust the process of spiritual unfolding to bring you to prayer when the time is right for you. At that time, you will feel a sense of attraction and ownership about your prayer life rather than a sense of obligation or oppression.

PRAYER:
A DEFINITION

What is prayer, and why does it seem difficult for us? We can think of prayer as *any practice that fosters or expresses our relationship with the sacred,* as we understand it. This can include meditation practices of all kinds. Early in my spiritual exploration, I refused to even say the word "prayer." Later, I wanted to use it, but the word would not come out of my mouth. I have since learned that many others have the same experiences and for

3

many different reasons. So if the word "prayer" puts you off, consider substituting "meditation," "reflection," or "contemplation." You may want to replace the language you read here with yours. Find a way to stay with it even though your vocabulary may be different.

OBSTACLES TO PRAYER

When we pray, we actively seek a relationship with the divine instead of passively waiting for a spiritual experience. Being in any relationship means we have to make ourselves vulnerable or visible. The idea of praying can feel threatening to us emotionally, possibly even physically.

For people who have histories of abuse and neglect, closeness is often linked to being hurt. If we "see" God as menacing or indifferent, we probably assume that a relationship with God will end in our being wounded or abandoned. The prospect of being close to God or a divine presence, something exceedingly more powerful and uncontrollable than any human, fills many of us with *terror.*

4

We may refuse to pray out of *defiance*. If we were forced to pray when we were children, we may have shunned it to retain autonomy. If we were brought up in a rigid religious tradition—or in a family that stressed only the rigid aspects of religion—we may deeply resent the dictates imposed on us. If we associate prayer with harshness and severity, we may feel our spiritual survival depends on avoiding it.

It can be enraging to remember the hypocrisy of people who were supposedly persons of prayer, the same people who hurt us or did not protect us. Our bitterness might be preventing us from praying. A woman now active in Adult Children of Alcoholics shares this story:

> All through grade school my father molested me. He would come into my room at night. I would pretend to be asleep, hoping he would go away. At first, he just fondled me, but as I got older, the abuse got worse and worse. When I was a teenager, he was having intercourse with me.

My grandmother lived in another town and we saw her two or three times a year. Three times I went to her and told her that Dad was touching me in bad ways at night. Each time she shook her head and said, "Take it to prayer, honey, just take it to prayer." At first, I did. I asked God to make my father stop molesting me. But he kept on, of course. I thought, "What good is prayer if God doesn't answer you?" I stopped praying for good when I was eleven.

The spiritual wound this woman suffered because of her grandmother's irresponsibility greatly compounded the emotional wound of her father's abuse. For many years, she directed her bitterness and rage at God more than at her father and grandmother for not answering her desperate pleas for help.

We may *despair* of any true benefit of prayer. Another daughter of an alcoholic father tells this story:

I would pray that my mom and dad wouldn't fight. He would go and sit at the bar until it closed. Then he'd come home, and she'd come home dog-tired from working the evening shift and he'd be drunk, and then they'd fight.

I can remember lying in my bed listening to them and praying to God to stop this fighting or praying that she would somehow get her act together and leave. Or that he would change or just have one sober day. Of course, it didn't stop until years later, when she divorced him. Somewhere along the line, I began to feel very punished. I got very angry with God.

In some families, prayer is thought of as foolish, and the person who prays is the object of contempt. *Self-preservation* might have kept us from prayer. Here's what happened to one man on a summer Sunday when he was about nine:

We were sitting out on the front porch,

which directly looked down on the sidewalk, watching families walk to church. There were two churches right across the street. As people walked by, Uncle Jack started calling out shaming comments, referring to them as the blind dummies, suckers for the Lutheran minister who was only after their money. The Lutherans, they were just basically stupid. But he would really tear into the Catholics. Catholics were crazy, believing in hocus-pocus. He would ask them how much holy water they were going to have to throw over their shoulders today to get saved. He was practically rabid.

In this kind of climate, a person would understandably go underground with prayer or stop altogether.

Many of us link prayer with *weakness* or *dependency.* For men in particular, asking a Higher Power for help can feel like a failure of manhood. The same man, now a recovering alcoholic, had this experience when he was sober three months:

I went to an AA roundup and a seventy-five-year-old man, thirty years sober, gave a talk. He made it clear that recovery is truly spiritual in nature and that without a spiritual awakening we don't recover. He made no bones about it and he talked about God. I was crying because I needed so much to hear this from a man and I had never heard it before. There were six thousand people at this hotel, but I found this guy and hugged him and thanked him.

My wife and I went out to breakfast the next morning. I told her, "I want to be a man who has a God." I cried when I said it to her. It felt so good to say it, but I could feel this embarrassment at the same time. Part of me was afraid that she would laugh at me. I wondered if she would still want to be with me now that she knew this was what I wanted.

Like many others, this man felt he had to risk both his masculinity and his marriage to become more openly spiritual.

Maybe we are *ashamed* because we don't know how to pray. As children, we probably prayed for *things:* bikes, dolls, good grades, home runs, new friends. As adults, we are quick to disown this "childish" part of ourselves, knowing no one gets things just by praying for them, but we may lack more sophisticated concepts or practices. Despite the current trendiness of spirituality, it is still very hard for many of us to talk with anyone—sometimes even our closest friends—about what we actually do when we pray. Consequently, we may hesitate when we need to ask for guidance and information to nurture our prayer life.

ADULTHOOD TRAUMA

If we have been through some trauma as adults, we may have great difficulty praying. A rape or battering may even cut us off from a well-established prayer life. Emotional pain—anger, shame, depression, despair—or physical injury may drain us of energy we need to stay connected to our deeper self and our Higher Power.

Sometimes our spontaneous prayer in the wake of a devastating experience is angry. We are angry about what we have suffered or lost, angry about being so powerless, and angry that God didn't protect us. Many of us learned early on that it isn't acceptable to be angry at God. If this is how we feel, we are probably cutting off the only voice that could speak freely and honestly to God.

On top of everything else, our family or religious community may insist that we pray for and forgive the person who did this to us. We are ashamed if we cannot bring ourselves to do this. We may accuse ourselves of having little faith or compassion.

For all these reasons, exploring and experimenting with prayer does not always come easily. When we reach the crossing place, some of us will step right in, while others will need to study the river for a long time. You can choose the method that works for you and take all the time you need to complete the crossing.

THE PRINCIPLES OF
RELATIONSHIP-BASED
PRAYER

In the best and healthiest relationships, our behavior is congruent with our inner values. Our conduct is based on empathy, understanding, and respect. Our primary concern is the well-being of the relationship and those in it.

When we pray, we must allow ourselves to be true to our values and temperament, to the voice of our spirit; we must allow ourselves to be congruent with our image of the sacred. Our prayer reflects unique strengths, fears, gifts, and style that we would bring to any good relationship. It will be based on our inner experience rather than the rules and expectations of others.

As our personal spiritual language becomes clearer and our voice stronger, we can bring more of our real self to transform our old images of God; we can perceive our relationship with our Higher Power afresh and discover new ways to relate. As our life brings us new opportunities and new challenges, we can stretch our prayer to accommodate the resulting changes.

Affirming prayer as a relationship, we open to the depth and the complexity of life's most vital connection. We avoid comparing ourselves with others or evaluating our "performance." We recognize that our difficulties in prayer are not a sign of trouble but rather an inevitable part of truly being *in relationship*. We accept the certainty that in prayer we will experience dejection and bliss, closeness and absence, challenge and ease, agony and comfort. We come to understand prayer as a process that evolves as we live and learn, not an achievement or a technique.

MY PRAYER PRACTICES

Before I suggest a route to prayer based on these principles, I think it might be helpful for you to know a little about the ways I pray so that you are aware of the personal context for my thoughts.

Like many people, I need variety in my prayer life. Frequently I pray spontaneously in wonder at the bounty of nature or in gratitude for people's kindness. Sometimes I ask for an extra measure of courage or compassion.

Sometimes I use *vipassana* meditation techniques, in which you focus on breathing and observing thoughts, feelings, and sensations without becoming engaged or trying to change them. The Passageway exercise (p. 29) will help you with this prayer practice. In his book *A Gradual Awakening,* Stephen Levine explains these techniques more extensively.

Sometimes in prayer I express complaints, fears, frustrations, questions, musings, appreciations. At times, I ask for guidance or help. Often I include others in my prayer, calling them to mind and expressing my feelings about them or their situations. When I have a major decision to make or am struggling with a serious dilemma in a relationship, I often bring it into prayer several times for a period of weeks. I have learned to trust that if I continue to seek wisdom, it will come to me. If verbal prayer appeals to you, you might enjoy Ann and Barry Ulanov's book *Primary Speech.*

In the warm months of the year, I sit for about half an hour several days a week under a young ash tree on a bench I made with bricks and a board. In my meditation I open myself to my surroundings, to everything I see, hear, feel, smell, and touch there. Meditating in the same spot week after week, seeing the same sights as the seasons change, holds a special wonder for me.

Often, I pray using passages from the Bible, the *Tao Te Ching,* or scriptures of other traditions. Sometimes poems or passages from novels are catalysts for prayer. I reflect on how the story touches me and why, what it says to me at this point in my life, and what it invites me to spiritually. Macrina Wiederkehr, in her book *A Tree Full of Angels,* brings this prayer practice to life.

During the growing season, one of my prayer practices is "surveying the estate," a ritual I adopted from my family. Once or twice a day, I visit the garden, noting changes since the previous day. I soak up through all my senses the vigor and beauty of the buds, blooms, and fruits, and of the birds, butterflies, and bees that live among them.

When I journal as a way to pray, I reflect on how I have felt the sacred in my life over the past few days, or weeks. Often, I sit quietly for a while before I begin to write and return to silence occasionally. Over time, journaling helps me recognize the constancy of my relationship with the sacred.

I have experimented with many other techniques and methods. Some of them I found oppressive, or foreign, or abrasive—so I abandoned them. Yet I know other people who embrace those very approaches enthusiastically because they fit for them. My ways to pray have stayed with me because they are compatible with who I am. As you begin, remember that prayer expresses your unique relationship with the divine.

ONE ROUTE TO A PRAYER LIFE

It is important to provide yourself with the essentials for spiritual growth, or prayer can become an experience of self-abuse or self-neglect. You don't want to go overboard with spiritual practices that are harmful to you, such as extended prayer retreats or severe fasting. You want to be able to trust yourself to make sound choices, not rigidly follow a particular style of prayer that doesn't bring you any closer to your Higher Power.

Kindly self-discipline allows you to focus your efforts and energy so you can experience real deepening in your connection with a holy presence. You will need this so you'll actually set aside time for prayer and choose gentle spiritual practices, so you'll explore one practice in depth rather than many superficially.

To grow in prayer, you need to create a climate of *safety* too. Feeling terrified or guarded is incompatible with the sense of relationship that is at the heart of praying. However many attempts it requires, experiment until you find a way to pray that lets you relax and be open to the experience.

Exploring prayer requires *empathy* and *trust*. If one practice makes you feel bad, try something else. If you find that a prayer practice chips away at your self-esteem, give yourself permission to try something else. If you learned about prayer from a faultfinding writer or teacher, find a more nurturing mentor. If you feel ashamed or scold yourself, take the time you need—minutes, hours, days, months—to establish an atmosphere of self-care.

Let this task *be* your prayer for a time. Make any change that will allow you to affirm and respect your efforts.

Finally, you need *dialogue* and *community* to sustain a life of prayer. You may seek out friends who encourage you and help you believe in your journey. You may find that a therapist or spiritual director can help you separate family issues from any impasse you reach when praying. And you may find it invaluable to talk with someone who already has a meaningful prayer life.

DEVELOPING A PRAYER LIFE

BECOME AWARE OF YOUR CONNECTION AND LONGING

The relational practice of prayer springs from the connection you already have with the sacred, from your longing to connect, and from your Higher Power's attempts to connect with you. To begin to pray, you need only to find the spark of relationship between yourself and the sacred and gently fan it until it begins to burn with a steady flame.

Begin by asking yourself, Where and when do I

spontaneously feel touched by the divine? You already identified some spiritual experiences.

Often, the first movement we make toward praying is prompted by restlessness or longing. You may hunger for more time for stillness and contemplation. Something may seem to be missing in your spiritual life. You may yearn for a more personal connection with God. At first, it may be difficult to translate this longing into words. Treat yourself with kindness and patience as you struggle for a better understanding. Keep in mind that this longing is, in itself, a spiritual experience. It is destined to be, in some ways, beyond human expression.

Nurture the Connection

Once you are aware of your natural style of spiritual communication, you can begin to foster the relationship. Your relationship with your Higher Power is, in many ways, like your other relationships. When you are drawn to someone, you arrange to spend more time together. Prayer is a way to give yourself time with your Higher Power.

Several years ago, I criticized myself for not being able to follow through on a strong desire to pray. A spiritual director told me the challenge was not for me to be more disciplined, but rather to change my lifestyle so it was compatible with praying. Seeing the truth in this, I gradually carved out a forty-five-minute block of time three mornings a week when I wouldn't be interrupted. While your rhythm of prayer is probably different from mine, you too will benefit from setting aside the time to pray.

As you get more comfortable with praying, you will probably want to learn more about different styles of prayer, such as Zen meditation, centering prayer, transcendental meditation, or *lectio divina* (prayer based on scripture passages). Talking with others about how they pray may help too.

Sometimes prayer is as simple as bringing your full attention to a mundane activity. Being truly present to what you are doing often discloses its spiritual nature. Here is what happened when one man decided to focus on work in his garden:

I was turning the compost pile—the leaves and grass and garbage from last season. You know, all the stuff we had thrown away. Over the winter and the early part of the spring it had all turned to dirt. Great stuff for the garden. I bent down and picked up a handful. I smelled it and it had the same scent that the air has right before a rain. It was so rich, so *ready*. Suddenly I found myself moved. To think that the stuff we had thrown away had become something that would make everything come alive! Standing there in the compost pile, I felt I was part of some ancient cycle that has been going on for millions of years.

Here are more examples of how people began to foster their spiritual connection that may help you select a style of praying:

John remembered how close he felt to God when he sang in the church choir as a boy. He recalled how touched he was by some of the hymns. He set aside a short block of private time once or twice a week. He would spend a few minutes quieting himself, and then he would sing a favorite hymn as soulfully as he could. Afterward he wrote about the experience.

❦

Joanie knew that flowers frequently touched her spirit. Each weekend she'd buy a big bouquet and take the time to arrange them, placing the flowers in several rooms of her home. As she did this, she would focus on the sensuous experience of handling, seeing, and smelling the flowers.

❦

Reflecting on his spiritual experiences, Paul remembered when he was ten and his father took him to a remote lake in the Rocky Mountains. They hiked about eight miles and camped near a lake for two nights, fishing and hiking during the day. For Paul, this experience of harmony—himself, his father, and the surroundings—was sacred. As an experiment, he wrote the story of that trip in his journal. Later, he shared it with his wife.

❧

Greg, a recovering alcoholic, felt himself drawn to the Eleventh Step of the Twelve Step programs, the one about improving conscious contact with God as we understand God. He went on a weekend retreat for men, where he journaled about the times he had felt in contact with his Higher Power and about people and activities that helped him to stay in contact now. He shared his new awareness with a spiritual director.

Whatever style of prayer you choose, check yourself to see whether the practice is helping you grow or is causing you to bring out survival strategies. If your prayers inspire growth, you will sense that you are receiving divine energy in return. Divine energy may come as new insight, or it may come in a dream. It may be a feeling of comfort or calm. It could be an experience of renewal or healing. Maybe it will be the gift of greater patience or compassion in a troubling situation.

You might need time to work on these first two steps toward praying, experimenting until you find a way that keeps you open to your true spiritual nature.

Overcome Obstacles

Nearly everyone encounters difficulties with prayer. Prayer leads us ever closer to the sacred. If we were abused, we may be terrified of intimacy with a Higher Power and wary of surrendering any control. We may be confused about what is normal in a relationship with the divine. Our religious background may have left us with images of God which imply that closeness to the divine will bring us only judgment or abandonment. Or it may have imposed on us oppressive and rigid rules about prayer.

While your journey toward a closer relationship with God shows your growing strength and health, it may be painful at times. Memories of traumatic events or emotions can occasionally intrude when you pray. If you get extremely restless or anxious during prayer, you may find yourself avoiding or neglecting a prayer practice you once enjoyed. You may find that you blame yourself when your practice falters, thinking you are stupid or incompetent. Even worse, you may see your difficulties in prayer as evidence that you are unworthy to be in a relationship with a Higher Power. These accusations are the remnants of past painful circumstances, not the truth about you.

Your task now is to learn more about why you have problems with praying. Perhaps the prayer practice you have chosen simply doesn't fit well for you. Many people struggled with meditation practices they thought would quiet them, but they only became more agitated and self-critical. When they found a more active style, their prayer came alive.

Your difficulties with prayer may have deep roots, however. By searching your feelings, memories, and thoughts during prayer, you might trace the connection to a traumatic experience. Most of what you need to know to resume your journey is probably just below your threshold of awareness. If you listen, you may hear the critical voices of clergy or parents. If you search, you may see old images of God. A woman raised in a fundamentalist church tells of her family-based struggles with prayer and meditation:

> As a young adult, I stopped attending church and had no spiritual life for about ten years, though I stayed in contact with my parents. In my late twenties, when I moved in with my boyfriend, my parents quoted Christian scripture to the effect that I was a sinner and would go to hell.
>
> I was hurt and angry, but I also felt

relieved by their rejection. It freed me so I could reexamine spirituality on my own. I began to practice yoga meditation and write in a journal every day. I was very rigid about this. If I missed a day, I criticized myself and "made up" for it the next day. I constantly felt that I wasn't doing it quite right, that whatever I did was never enough. Though I was miserable during meditation, I was determined to try harder.

One day a friend who had known me since high school listened to my struggles with meditation. She pointed out that I sounded just like my parents: compulsive, rigid, harsh, never good enough. I burst into tears. In trying so hard to make a break from my parents' religious oppression, I had unknowingly continued to oppress myself. That was why I was so stuck.

Sometimes just becoming aware of how you have been blocked will clear the way to a renewed connection with the sacred. However, you may find that while you understand how you are trapped, you have no idea how to escape. Sometimes talking with a partner or a friend can reveal a way out. You might even need the help of a therapist or spiritual director to regain your freedom.

As you reflect on your experiences in prayer, remember that you are the ultimate authority on what's best for you. All your options are always open. Don't force yourself to continue with any prayer style. You can take a break for as long as you need to learn more or to reduce your anxiety. You don't even need to know the reasons for your pain or explain them to anyone before you make a change.

When you are ready to go ahead again with new insight about your own prayer, you will have completed one stage of your journey. Each new stage you go through will deepen your understanding, and your practice of prayer will grow in this spiral pattern.

Here you can explore your experiences with prayer and those who pray. Before you do the

Passageway exercise, take a few minutes to look over the Exploration and Discovery section. You may decide to complete one or both of the exercises. For now, choose the one you would like to do first.

❧

PASSAGEWAY

Settle into a position that allows you to be comfortable but alert. When you are ready...

Bring your awareness to your breathing. ❧ Notice whether it is deep or shallow ❧ fast or slow. ❧ Be aware of your breath as it moves in ❧ and out of your body. ❧ See if you can notice your breathing without trying to change it. ❧ Let your breath become the focus of your attention ❧ gentle and unforced. ❧ Notice how your breath feels going in ❧ and out ❧ in ❧ and out.

When your attention wanders away from your breathing, be aware of where it has gone, without following it. ❧ Notice if you are planning ❦ remembering ❦ feeling ❦ hearing ❦ seeing. ❦ Simply notice where your energy is focused. ❦ Then gently bring it back to your breath ❦ without criticism. ❦ Just gently return to your breath ❦ breathing in ❦ and breathing out ❦ in ❦ and out.

Let your breath be the place of return for you. If your mind wanders off, notice where it has gone and come back to your breath, ❦ breathing in and breathing out ❦ in ❦ and out ❦ in ❦ and out. ❦

Notice more and more subtle sensations of breathing, ❦ the air moving in ❦ and out ❦ through your nose ❦ your chest rising ❦ and falling ❦ your abdomen expanding ❦ and contracting. ❦ Be aware of your breath as it moves in and out. ❦ If you notice your mind has wandered, simply note where it has gone, without following it, and gently bring your attention back to the centering point of your breath ❦ back to the focus point. ❦ Breathe in ❦ and out ❦ with no demand for concentration ❦ no criticism for a shift in focus. ❦

Simply notice and return to your breath. ❧ Breathe in and out ❧ in ❧ and out. ❧ Breathe in ❧ and out ❧ in ❧ and out. ❧ Notice the details of your breathing ❧ and the movements of your attention. ❧ Notice without following. ❧ Simply observe the movements of your attention ❧ and return to the centering point of your breath without criticism. ❧ Just breathe in and breathe out ❧ noticing the flow of air in ❧ and out. ❧ Continue breathing in ❧ and out ❧ for a few more minutes ❧ in ❧ and out. ❧

Now gently come back to the place where you are sitting. ❧ Let yourself return to the room and to the objects in it. Be fully aware of your surroundings.

When you are ready, go on to the Exploration and Discovery section.

EXPLORATION AND DISCOVERY

Here you will explore your past and present relationship with prayer. Give yourself the freedom to write or draw anything that comes to you, without judging or censoring yourself. You need not be sensible, logical, or orderly. Let yourself be as spontaneous, creative, and messy as you like.

You may have intense emotions in response to the exercises. If you do, take time to identify and experience each feeling. Allow the emotion to give you important information about your relationship with the sacred.

EXERCISE 1:
EXPLORING YOUR ASSOCIATIONS
WITH THE WORD "PRAYER"

To do this exercise, you need a large piece of paper (11" x 17" inches or larger is best) and a pen. You may be more expressive if you use colored markers. For a better idea of the exercise, look at the example on the next page.

In the center of the paper, write PRAYER. Circle it. Now, as quickly as you can, write down any word you associate with prayer. Circle each word you write and connect it to the center circle with a line. You can include feelings, memories,

32

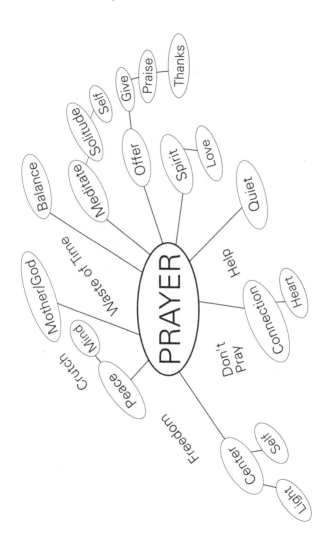

names, ideas, or anything else that can be expressed in one or two words. Let the process flow freely. Do not stop to analyze. As you write a word, you will probably notice that related words come to you. Circle each and connect it to the word that triggered it. Keep going; put down whatever comes to you and wherever there is open space. Continue until you run out of words. ✍

Now look at your diagram. As you do, a few more words will probably occur to you. If so, add them to the diagram. ✍

Now take a break. You might want to stretch or make yourself a cup of tea. Give your mind a chance to rest. When you are ready, take another look at the diagram. Be aware of any connections or relationships that stand out. Notice anything that seems especially important or captivating. Take five or ten minutes (no more) to write about anything your diagram or the exercise has brought to your attention. Be spontaneous. Let the writing take any form that fits for you at the moment. ✍

When you have finished, again rest awhile.
Then go over what you have written. How do you
feel when you read it? If it makes you think of anything else, make a note of it. ✍

You might find these exercises helpful too:

1. Choose one word from your diagram. Make
   it the center of another diagram and explore
   it the same way you did with the word
   "prayer."
2. Write in more detail about any feeling or
   memory that has surfaced during this exercise.

EXERCISE 2:
YOUR HISTORY OF PRAYER
AND MEDITATION

This exercise is an inventory to help you identify
the role of prayer and meditation in your life from
your early childhood to the present. You may want
to work on it over a period of time rather than trying to do it all in one sitting.

Begin with several pages, one for each phase of

your life. For example, you may want to use five-year segments. Or you may divide your history into preschool, grade school, junior high, high school, and so on. Or you may organize it in some other way that is meaningful to you.

Begin with any phase of your life. Write down anything you remember about prayer or meditation during that period. How did you pray (if at all)? If you didn't pray, why not? How did you meditate (if at all)? If you didn't meditate, why not? What did you learn about prayer at this age? What did you believe about it? What were your struggles or questions about prayer? About meditation? With whom do you associate prayer or meditation at this age? How do the events of this period affect your prayer now?

Let these questions be guides for you. If other events or feelings are more important, write about them instead. Gradually record your history of prayer and meditation in each segment of your life. You may find that memories from one segment spark memories from another, and you may go back and forth between the pages. ✍

When you have filled in everything you can, set aside a block of time to read everything you have written. When you read it, write your feelings, insights, and questions in your journal. ✍

Here are some more ideas to try:

- Share your history—or certain parts of it—with a friend, partner, sponsor, therapist, or spiritual director.
- Identify gaps or questions you have about your childhood that could relate to your background on prayer. Then gather more information by asking family members or others to help fill in the gaps.

❧

REFLECTION AND INTEGRATION

You've explored your relationship with prayer and meditation in some depth. Here you can reflect on everything you have learned. Consider using the Passageway exercise to re-center yourself in preparation for this section.

Begin by taking a block of time to look over your journal entries and drawings. Look for patterns in your history, for threads of continuity. Look for abrupt breaks or shifts as well. Be alert to relationships between events and persons that may not have been obvious before. Check to see whether anything is missing.

As you go, make a few notes about your observations. Also note any questions that surface. ✍

Now sit quietly for a time. Notice any new thoughts, ideas, or questions you may have about prayer. Write about or draw them in any way that feels right to you. ✍

You may find it helpful to record your responses to the following questions:

- How would you describe your relationship with prayer now?
- Would you like to change your feelings about praying in any way? If so, how? Be specific.
- What stands in your way as you consider

making changes in your prayer life? List ideas, feelings, experiences, persons, lifestyle choices.

- What kind of help or guidance do you need (if any) to "grow" your prayer life? What are some possible sources of help? Are you willing at this time to ask for it? If not, why not?

- Who would support you in becoming a person of prayer? Who might block your growth in that direction?

- Would you like to share some of what you have discovered with anyone? Name some people who would be receptive and respectful. You could also note what you would like to share with each of them.

- Is there anything you've learned that you would like to explore in more depth, either on your own or with someone else? Learn more about? Experiment with? Make a note of it, and make plans to act on it.

In choosing to complete these exercises, you have begun the crossing that will lead you to a deeper and richer spiritual life. The experience may have freed you from ideas or feelings that no longer fit. If you are enthusiastic, you may want to use your journal to follow some of the threads you have found or seek others who might join you in cultivating prayer.

The exercises may have been challenging or painful for you. If you feel lost or confused, you may find it helpful to meet with a spiritual guide or member of the clergy. If you have discovered that your relationship with your Higher Power is tangled up with your painful history, a therapist may be able to be of help. Whatever your next steps, remember that since they are aimed at a closer relationship with your Higher Power, they are in themselves a form of prayer.

Like all other relationships, your relationship with the sacred through prayer will be constantly evolving for as long as you live. It would be so much simpler if we could just find one way to pray that would work forever! But if we are growing, our life prods us, calls us, to deeper self-awareness. It teaches us how to be more loving and steadfast in our relationships. It brings us new encounters with the divine. All these gifts of life naturally change the form and content of our prayer. As you continue to explore and deepen your prayer, you can celebrate change as a sign that you're growing.

ABOUT THE AUTHOR

Peg Thompson, Ph.D., offers psychotherapy, spiritual direction, consultation, and training services through her private practice in St. Paul, Minnesota. She is the author of *Finding Your Own Spiritual Path: An Everyday Guidebook*, published by Hazelden (October 1994). She also teaches a course on religious and spiritual development at two Twin Cities graduate schools. When not working, she can often be found tending her garden or fishing in a trout stream. She lives with her partner and their two dogs in a rural setting near the Twin Cities.